Prepping: Survival Basics

By: Tom Eckerd

Special Request

Thank you for purchasing our book and supporting our Ministry. We have a Special Request for those that have purchased this book on the Kindle platform. We wanted to make you aware that Amazon's Kindle platform pays per pages "read". Our Special Request is that if you appreciate our Ministry's efforts to put out books such as this or if you would simply like to support our Ministry's work to please scroll to the back of the book, even if you don't "read" the book right away. This is how we will get paid through the paid per pages criteria.

We all lead such busy lives nowadays and can get side tracked so easily please take a moment to support us now by allowing us to be paid by scrolling to the end of the book – Then go back and read it at your leisure.

We deeply appreciate Your support and know that God will Bless You as You have Blessed this Ministry.

Dedication

This book is dedicated to all the members of the American Christian Defense Alliance as well as my Lord and Savior Jesus Christ who laid down His life and rose again that I might have eternal life and be with the father in Heaven.

Forward

First off thank you for purchasing our book, "Prepping: Survival Basics". We deeply appreciate your patronage and support.

In this book we lay the foundations for the average person to start prepping and to understand the survival basics. We cover some of the more critical aspects of prepping to help expedite the probability of your survival. This book will help jumpstart your education in prepping and survival.

This book will also help you to better understand what's involved in various kits and how things are interrelated when it comes to your survival. We don't just plan for one thing, we planned for everything.

We hope you will enjoy this book and leave us a positive rating as it tremendously helps us reach more people.

Table of Contents

Chapter 1: Educate Yourself

Educating yourself is like investing in yourself and your family for the future. The more that you educate yourself on things like being prepared and survival the better off you and your family will be. Nowadays college students can spend anywhere from $30,000.00 to $150,000.00 for a college education - whether it's a lawyer, teacher, or doctor Though these professions may have certain intrinsic values to them, if you were any one of those people in those particular professions in the middle of the forest would you be able to survive?

If your profession that you spent thousands of dollars educating yourself on is pointless when it comes to actual physical survival skills you need to re-educate yourself now with the proper survival skills.

If you were willing to spend thousands of dollars on a college education that honestly isn't worth that much nowadays and will not prepare you or your family to survive in the middle of nowhere - you got to ask yourself what is the point. Now what would happen if you invested the same amount of money you spent to go to college on being prepared?

I believe that the Native American Indians had it right - everyone was trained in particular skills that enabled them to live off of the land in a harmonious type of way without destroying it but living in balance. If you spent thousands of dollars on a skill, on a trade, or on a degree and you don't have the skills necessary still to survive off the land it's time to reinvest in educating yourself and gain these viable lifesaving skills.

Now thankfully you still have time to learn through books like this whether online or physically – but time is running out quickly.

Additionally with the advent of the Internet and companies like You Tube there is a tremendous amount of resources available free of charge or with books like this at a minimum cost. The amount of value that you can get from one awesome book or one great video that can literally give you the knowledge to save you or your family member's life – how can you honestly put a price tag on that? It's like asking how much is your life worth, how much is your family's life worth – thankfully most of this knowledge can be picked up by investing more time than money.

I would encourage everyone out there to get a small collection of books that they're actually going to read as well as some small manuals with specific detailed information that you put in your bug out bag just in case you forget a particular skill to have the book as a resource. In fact I would say every bug out bag should probably have two books at least in them, a King James Version Bible and a survival manual.

In addition to small group of books I would also encourage you to create a You Tube account and learn how to develop play list. Then start adding videos to your playlist that teach you solid information on key areas like shelter building, water purification, fire building, knife selection, etc.

All of this education is great but much like your gear if you don't test it out prior to needing it you're not going to know if it works and you may be up that proverbial river without a paddle. It's absolutely critical to get out on whatever land you plan to survive on and test the knowledge that you have acquired through reading and observing – it's what we call "Dirt Time".

After reading and observing the next logical step is doing, practicing the knowledge that you have learned. Thus after practicing that knowledge turns into wisdom and that wisdom turns into practical application of learned skills.

The American Christian Defense Alliance, Inc. outdoor ministry of the Burning Bush Survival and Preparedness School is currently also in the development of various courses to help prepare you. Please visit our website and sign up for a mailing list for future updates.

Chapter 2: Core Foundations

In chapter 2 we will cover some of the meat and potatoes of prepping survival basics. Please pay close attention to the information in the section as it is of a critical nature.

Selecting a Survival Knife

Of all your survival equipment, the single most important piece (besides your Bible) is a good knife. Many experts have agreed that if they had to pick only one piece of equipment to use, it would be their knife. That makes sense really, as you can make much of the rest of what you need out of what nature provides you, if you have a knife to work with. No other single piece of equipment does more.

The question then becomes, what sort of knife should you buy? There are a plethora of knives available on the market, available for a wide range of prices and with a large range of options to choose from.

There are even knives marketed as survival knives, which contain all sorts of extra equipment to help you survive. So, what's the best?

First of all, this is one place where quality counts more than anything else. If you are going to depend on a knife to help you survive, you need one that is going to hold up under the strain of heavy use, without a risk of it breaking and hopefully with the ability to maintain a good, sharp edge.

With that being our criteria, the first thing to consider is the knife's construction. You want a fixed-blade knife, rather than a folding one. Folding knives can break more easily and the lock can slip at an inopportune moment, causing a serious injury. A folding knife is fine as a backup, but your primary knife should be fixed-blade.

The blade needs to have a full tang. This refers to the part of the blade that extends back through the handle.

Manufacturers of cheap knives use partial tangs to save money. But the handle is likely to break right at the end of the tang, when the knife is subject to extreme pressure, leaving you with a blade that doesn't have a handle. That's awfully hard to work with.

I would recommend a blade style that gives you a strong point, as the point is the most fragile part of the blade. Drop point knives are pretty good for this, as well as tonto blades. I personally like clip point knives a lot, because you get a sharper point; but those are not as good for survival knives. The same can be said for dagger point knives. Besides, you don't need a fighting knife as a survival knife, you need a working tool.

The other main issue is the steel that the knife is made of. Most commercially made knives today are made of some sort of stainless steel. That is nice in that it doesn't rust, but stainless steel doesn't hold an edge like high-carbon steel does.

The best knives have been made of high-carbon steel for centuries.

Some of the best high-carbon steel comes out of Solingen, Germany. This town is known for their knives, most of which are kitchen knives. However, there are a few companies in Solingen who produce outdoor knives.

Another very popular option is true Damascus steel. This is actually a layered laminate of high-carbon steel and a softer spring steel. The two together provide an excellent edge, while keeping the knife from becoming brittle. High-carbon steel by itself is so hard, that it can be brittle at times. Damascus steel is the one truly obvious steel option, because its layers cause a striped pattern in the knife's blade.

But other than Damascus steel, it's very hard to tell the difference between other types of steel. Not all manufacturers will give you that information, essentially expecting you to trust them for the selection of a good steel for your knife.

There are a number of companies who produce excellent knives. It seems that each survival expert has their favorite. ESSE, Tops, Cold Steel, and Becker are popular brands, all three of which specialize in survival and combat knives. The old standbys of K-Bar and Gerber are good choices as well; especially for people who don't want to spend as much money.

Whatever brand you ultimately choose, realize that you're not going to get a quality knife at a bargain basement price. Cheap knives are just that... cheap. Most especially, they use cheap steel, which won't hold an edge. To get a good knife, you're going to have to spend some money; somewhere between $70 and $200.

Avoid knives with a built-in saw blade, unless the saw blade is on the back side of the knife.
A two inch long saw blade isn't going to accomplish much for you and it's going to shorten the knife's effective blade, reducing what you can do with it.

You should also avoid "gimmick" knives, which are selling you a survival kit in a knife. Remember, to give you the other stuff, they have to reduce the cost of the knife. That's done by using cheaper steel.

Shelter

Regardless of whether you're trying to make your way home after a disaster, trying to bug out after a disaster, or just trying to make your way out after being lost in the wilderness, shelter is going to be an important factor.
Shelter is one of the things we use to protect ourselves from the weather and maintain our body heat, making it one of our most important survival priorities.

The biggest killer in the wild is hypothermia, the loss of body heat. This can happen year-round, as the ambient air temperature is normally lower than our body's temperature. When we get wet, either through excessive sweating, rain or from falling in a body of water, our bodies shed heat rapidly. Without shelter, it doesn't take long for hypothermia to set in.

That's why it's important to always carry some sort of shelter materials in your bug out bag or EDC bag (everyday carry bag). It doesn't take much; you don't need an expensive backpacking tent. A simple tarp and some cordage will help you make a decent shelter in a pinch.

But more important than the materials you are carrying is to start with what nature offers. There are a lot of things that can be used for shelter, when in the wild. Some can be used as they are, while others may need to be improved with the help of your tarp and cordage. Either way, starting with what nature provides makes the job easier.

So, what sorts of things can you look for in nature to use as shelter? Caves – Check to make sure they are unoccupied, before going in. Rock Outcroppings – They will often have places where two or three rocks have a space between them which can quickly be converted to a cave. Undercut Embankments – Rivers or flash floods can undercut an embankment, creating a wide but shallow cave.

With a wind screen in front and a fire in-between, this makes a comfortable shelter.

Overturned Trees – The space below the tree can be cleaned out for a shelter or the root mass makes a good back wall for a shelter. Thickets of Trees – Often saplings will grow close enough together to create a hidden spot which blocks off the wind.

You might have to cut a few saplings out of the middle and string your tarp overhead, but it will provide a great windbreak. Other than the caves, you'll have to make some modifications in pretty much all these cases.
That's where your tarp and cordage come in. The tarp can either be used as a roof or as walls, depending on the needs of your particular shelter.

Another great material that you can find in the wild is to use tree branches. Layered against the side of the shelter or on the roof, they shed rain well and provide good resistance to break up the wind.

The key here, more than anything, is being able to improvise. Simply opening your eyes and seeing what nature has already created is the first step in creating any shelter. Then, it's just a matter of figuring out how to make that shelter more rain and wind proof, as well as where you can place your fire to keep you warm.

Fire

Fire has to be one of the most useful tools that God has given mankind. While our main use of fire is to help keep us warm, it goes beyond that in meeting our needs. Fire also provides us with light, a means of cooking our food and even a way of purifying water. All this makes fire an essential for survival. While we could theoretically survive without it, trying to do so requires much more effort than building and maintaining the fire does. So, it ultimately makes more sense to have a fire as a part of any survival effort, than not to have it. Actually, it's one of the first things we should do.

If you've ever watched someone try to start a fire, who doesn't know what they're doing, you should have a pretty good appreciation of the difficulty involved. If we were to analyze the fire starting methodology of these people, we'd probably quickly encounter that they are causing much of their own problem. Most specifically, they aren't working their way up through the different types of flammable materials correctly.

What do I mean by that? I mean starting with tinder, working your way up to kindling and then to the fuel for your fire. Most of the time, they try to jump from tinder to fuel or sometimes from a match to fuel. What's the difference between these things? Tinder consists of things that will catch fire easily from one match or other fire starter. You can include dry grass, newspaper, char-cloth, dryer lint and dry moss in this category. Every fire needs tinder to get it started.

Kindling is small flammable material that will burn longer than the rapid-burning tinder and allow the flame to grow so that it will ultimately catch the fuel on fire. Usually, we're talking about sticks the diameter of your finger here. Larger sticks can be used, if they are made into a "fuzz stick."

Fuel is what your fire is going to burn to provide you with heat. Typically, we're talking about pieces about the diameter of your arm. This gives a nice balance between catching fire fairly easily and not burning too quickly. About the only time you want chunks of wood larger than this, is if you are setting the fire up to burn through the night.

These three types of material need to be set up in a teepee or pyramid structure, so that the burning tinder can catch the kindling on fire and then the kindling can catch the fuel on fire. As flame, like any other heat rises, this is typically done by putting the tinder on the bottom, with the kindling above it and the fuel forming the outer shell.

There are many ways you can provide an initial spark, ember or flame to the fuel, in order to start a fire. Survival instructors collect fire starting methods like some people collect baseball cards. But if you have simple fire starters, you might want to use them. This usually means waterproof matches or a butane lighter.

A lighter is probably the best single fire starter you can carry. A typical lighter will start about 1,000 fires, if it is used carefully and not wasted. It's compact, fairly water resistant and reliable. The only problem is that it won't work in cold weather. But to solve this problem, you can keep the lighter inside your clothing to keep it warm.

Most survival instructors say you should carry two primary and two secondary forms of fire starting. Lighters and matches are the primary means. Things like metal matches, Ferro Rods, magnifying glasses, 0000 steel wool and a battery, and a bow drill all fall into the category.

Other than for practice, you really only want to use one of these secondary methods in the case where you don't have your primary methods. I prefer to carry two lighters, one of which is totally waterproof, rather than mess with those other methods (although I have them too).

One other thing you should always carry for starting a fire is an accelerant. This is something, usually chemical, which will burn readily.

While the term "accelerant" is normally used in association with arson, it's the correct term to use in this case as well. If you do a search online for "fire starters" you'll find some of these, along with things like the Metal Match and Ferro Rod. Some of the best are cube shaped and individually wrapped.

A fire accelerant is especially useful when it is wet out. You really don't want to use them all the time, but if it is raining, you'll be glad you have one.

You can make your own as well, by working petroleum jelly into cotton balls. One cotton ball, treated in this way, will burn for over three minutes, making it great for getting a stubborn fire started.

Water

Water is one of the key elements to life and survival. During a crisis situation, SHTF, or your Bug Out finding and making potable water is a must. It's important to understand the time frame that your body has for needing water. Your body runs best when properly hydrated each and every day. Lack of hydration will cause lack of focus and lack of focus will cause poor decisions to be made – it's not just physical thing - your body needing water.

Water affects everything. Your body can only survive approximately 3 days without water. That being said it's vital to understand how to find water and how to make it drinkable.

There lots of filters and purifiers on the market today each one having its own unique benefits and disadvantages. Check our website for current recommendations. However, having a steel container to boil water in will go a long way to making water potable.

Now considering that the mentality and the plan that God has for us is to escape and evade we might not be in a position in which fire would be such a good idea. There are lots of ways to hide a fire such as a Dakota fire pit but in all reality sometimes it's better not to take the chance and build a fire while being hunted. You have to remember, even if they can't see your fire they might be able to smell your smoke or see a smoke signal. If you built a fire close to the thick evergreen tree you might be able to hide the smoke for those around but it's still not a good idea while in escape and evade mode.

Therefore, that's when certain water filters water purifiers come in the play. They enable you to have fresh clean drinking potable water without the need of the fire – a significant tactical advantage for you while on the run. Again check our website for the most updated list of recommendations.

When trying to acquire up in the Surrey water for survival as you bug out there a few options. You could attempt to catch water with a tarp or poncho and drain that water into a steel container and boil it. The fire is not an option that you could still drain the water into your container; however, this is where you would need something similar to a Life Straw (which is a lightweight filter that you drink out of).

Another option for the Christian Prepper would be to read the terrain to determine if there is a stream, Creek or other potential body of water in the local vicinity. Obviously all water flows downhill so as you continue to move down there is a greater chance to find water.

This is where being prepared and having foresight comes into play. If you have prepared your bug out bag appropriately prior to needing it you should have your water containers already filled as well as the appropriate necessities to process water appropriately for safe consumption. Another great option is water tabs.

Now for those with a thyroid condition you may want to watch your iodine consumption. However, these are a great option as they are the latest option available and can be thrown into any pocket or kit. Just remember you're still good and need a steel container I cannot over emphasize the importance of the steel container. I should also mention that it's important to have a wide mouth steel container, as this will give you more options and make your life just a little bit easier on the go.

Food

Everything has it's purpose in your systems and Long Term Food Storage is no different. That being said, I would also say that All LTFS is only a backup to other backups you have in place.

You should strive to live a life in which you produce your own food or source it directly from nature - Don't rely on others to feed you, chances are you will no doubt starve at a rapid rate.

Long Term Food Storage should not be confused with food that you utilize in your Bug Out Bag / Go Bag or Bug Out Vehicle or in a Cache'. This is not the intended purpose for LTFS.

For these systems you should consider MREs (Meals Ready to Eat) and Mainstay Food Ration Bars (3600 Cal.). Both also make great additions to any cache and do not require any water to actually cook or produce . . . Unlike the Long Term Food Storage options which will require water to make.

Grab & Go should be just that to limit the amount of extra worry in your food preparations. Furthermore, take time to explore, study, and learn about wild edibles - this knowledge alone could save your life.

Grab & Go Options (No Preparation Needed) - Self life of 5-7 Years

MREs (Meals Ready-to-Eat)
Mainstay Food Rations (3600 Cal)

LTFS = Long Term Food Storage

There are a lot of options out there for anyone when it comes to Long Term Food Storage (LTFS) including Do It Yourself Options such as canning or vacuum sealing your own food. If your resources and abilities permit it this is the cheapest option to get the most bang for your buck. Yet when you need to Bug Out all that food stays right there unless you have it cached in a safe location. LTFS Companies that offer who have freeze dried food in buckets help with the transportation or transition of such food but it still is in a bucket so you can't bring it when you go on foot.

Now I've done the math here and for some of the LTFS options or plans if you would you could purchase Grab & Go Back Packing Options such as Backpackers Pantry. I recently did just that.

One thing that really gets to me is how the so called LTFS business doesn't include any real meat in their meals - What do you see out there? Pasta, Soups, Rice, Some Beans, and a whole lot of Cheese. I'm not sure about anyone else but I keep thinking of the old Wendy's commercial when they say, "Where the Beef"

99% of the time you have to purchase the meat separately and it's ridiculous in price, so what's another way to move forward with a practical plan that gives you the protein you will need in a stressful situation? Backpackers Pantry or another similar option – and with these when you Bug Out they come with you, well at least some of it – Try that will a 50lbs of Rice, good luck, lol. Also go as organic and healthy as possible - if you put "Crap" in your body you literally will get "Crap" out.

Can goods are another great way to get protein on the cheap, relatively speaking that is. Check out your local wholesale club - We shop at BJs and they are doing a great job moving to more organic items. However, again just remember you're not going to throw a bunch of can goods in your Bug Out Bag, it's just too heavy.

Now I don't want you to walk away thinking that long-term food storage is a waste of time, it's not. You don't know what situations can take place and for that reason alone you should have long-term food storage. The Word of God says no one knows the day or the hour but we are able to read the seasons – that being said is good to plan accordingly. Remember there will be famine throughout the land prior, I repeat prior to us being hated and persecuted and martyred. So to help us endure and whether the storm it's critical to have enough food stored up both at your house and other various locations.

How much food? Well that honestly depends on the size of your family, on how long you desire to feed them - six months, a year, or maybe five years. As a Christian Prepper I would recommend at least four years' worth of food to be stored up if at all financially possible. I would recommend freeze-dried as the best option. Freeze-dried food does carry a higher price point but you are receiving all the nutrients unlike the dehydrated foods.

Long Term Food Storage does have its place in the Christian Preppers life especially if you have a Bug Out Retreat or if you don't plan to Bug Out. For the Christian Prepper who has the resources it would be a great idea to purchase LTFS and Cache it in various places. Keep in mind with any LTFS Company you have to Read the Fine Print and know what to look for. There is an Art and a Science to buying LTFS. Our organization does support some LTFS as an option and is partnering with selected companies that provide the greatest value and benefits to those we serve. Check our website for the latest reviews on companies and their products.

Your stockpile of food for you and your family should consist of a multi layered system where options such as bugging out and bugging in are considered. Additionally, caches of preparations and food along commonly travel routes and approximately 5 miles away from your home should be considered as vital links in your overall survival plan.

Chapter 3: Personal Care

In the previous chapter I briefly discussed proper food and water, in this chapter we will cover personal care as it relates to bugging out. Additionally we will cover hygiene while bugging out and medical training you should receive prior to having to bug out.

Hygiene and Personal Care

Hygiene and personal care while bugging out is something of critical importance. Hygiene and personal care is the number one issue taking people out worldwide. Even more than war improper hygiene and personal care is one of the fastest ways to take you and your family out of the game. Therefore it's important to plan and prep accordingly. Those with special needs should take great care and caution in the planning as medications and urgent care most likely will not be available. There are options to stock up on antibiotics if that's something you are in need of through the use of fish antibiotics.

However, use at your own discretion and accordingly to all applicable laws.

The label itself will tell you this is only for fish. A great Christian Prepper who just also happens to be a nurse did a great video on this a while back just search out the Patriot Nurse on YouTube. She does a lot of great videos on medical preparedness and does offer classes throughout the country. If you do stop by and visit her let her know you found her through our book.

One of the main things to throw into your bug out bag is a personal care kit. This kit should include things such as tweezers, toenail clippers, a pair of scissors, a bandanna and other individual specific hygiene items. Again remember stores are not open so what you have is what you have and you need to be able to improvise with what you bring. Women especially should take note of this and plan accordingly to deal with her menstrual cycle.

Medical Training

At the bare minimum every adult should be trained in First Aid and CPR. Medical training should be completed prior to any situation taking place if at all possible.
Do not put off medical training, as you do not know when a situation will take place in which you may need this particular training. I personally am an American Red Cross Instructor and have taught numerous individuals first aid and CPR classes at different places I've worked. I continue to offer training to those within our organization.

This training is on a first-come first serve basis and is limited to 10 people per class. In the future the American Christian defense Alliance, Inc. hopes to offer further courses from the American Red Cross. Their training is top-notch and very professional.

Chapter 4: Kits & Bags

If you spend any time at all around prepping or survivalist circles, you're going to end up hearing people talk about their various types of kits and bags. That's basically because of the importance of having everything you need with you to survive is so critical. While it is theoretically possible to survive without a kit, it is infinitely harder and requires much more knowledge about survival. Jesus Himself told His Disciples to go sell what you have and buy a bag . . .

Luke: 22: 35-38:
(35) And He said to them, "When I sent you without money bag, knapsack, and sandals, did you lack anything?" so they said, "Nothing." (36) Then He said to them, "But now, he who has a money bag, let him take it, and likewise a knapsack; and he who has no sword, let him sell his garment and buy one. (37) For I say to you that this which is written must still be accomplished in Me: 'And He was numbered with the transgressors. For the things concerning Me have an end." (38) So they said, "Lord, look, here are two swords." And He said to them, "It is enough."

If you're going to build a kit, you need to do it in the best possible way. The problem for many people is trying to figure out what all those different bag names mean and what you actually need to have in them so you can survive. So, let's look at the various types of kits and bags you might encounter:

Survival kit - This is a small, portable kit, usually packed into something the size of a hardcover book or smaller. The idea is to have something with you at all times, that gives you the essentials for survival. Many people carry these while hiking, or keep one in their car.

EDC Bag (Everyday Carry Bag) - The EDC is intended to give you everything you would need to have with you, if a disaster happened and you were away from home. As such, it needs to cover a lot of ground in a fairly small package. A typical EDC is roughly the size of a lunch box, although the shape can vary greatly. In many cases, people add non-essential, but useful things to their EDC, such as stamps, safety pins, and a phone charger.

Get Home Bag - The idea behind a get home bag is to provide you with enough urban survival equipment and a little food, so that you can make it home from work, in the event of a disaster. The assumption is that you would have to walk, so a get home bag may even include a good pair of walking shoes. Properly done, a EDC can also be used as a get home bag.

But Out Bag (BOB) - Sometimes called a 72-hour bag, this is what you would use if you determine you need to bug out and get away from home to survive a disaster. Different people's BOB will hold different equipment, depending on their bug out plan. It is intended to get you to your survival shelter, whether that is in another city, a cabin in the woods, or if you are going to live off the land. Obviously, if you're going to live off the land, you need more survival gear.

Inch Bag - This is the extreme version of a bug out bag, for those who intend to live off the land for the rest of their lives. Inch stands for "I'm never coming back." As the name implies, that means you're going to need a lot of gear to make it through. Regardless of the type of bag, they all have to provide for the basic survival needs, which are:

- A way to maintain your body temperature
- Clean water
- Food
- Fire
- Self-defense
- First-aid

Portability is an important consideration. You can't assume that you'll be able to use your car. Roads may be impassible, so you'll have to head out on foot. If that's the case, you want your kit or bag to be something that you can take with you.

That means putting it into a portable pack, such as a backpack or over-the-shoulder bag that you can actually carry. Therefore, you also need to consider how much weight you can carry, especially in the cases of the bug out bag and inch bag.

Chapter 5: The EDC

What is an Every Day Carry (EDC)? Disasters, like babies being born, show up on when they want, not when we want. That generally means at the most inopportune times. Somethings probably not going to happen when you're at your home and have just finished repacking your bug-out bag. It'll happen when you least expect it and aren't anywhere near your survival equipment.

That's why you need to be carrying some basic things with you every single day. If you walk out your door, you need to have enough with you to make it back home. Now, that doesn't mean you need to take your bug out bag with you, but it does mean that you need some things.

The idea of Ever Day Carry (EDC) is to have the essentials with you. We can break this down into two levels; the essentials that you carry on your person and those that you carry in an EDC bag.

The difference is, there are times when you will put your EDC bag down, such as while you are at work. Most would probably leave their EDC bag in the car while working; but the items you carry on your person are those that you might need in a matter of seconds, rather than minutes.

So, what are these items that you might need in seconds?

- Pistol with extra ammo (not only to defend yourself, but to defend others; believers should take a stand to protect the weak)
- Good knife and/or multi-tool with a knife blade
- Fire starter (a butane lighter works well for this)
- Flashlight
- Cash
- Keys
- Smartphone (have survival manuals and an electronic Bible in memory)
- Tactical pen (a pen which can also be used as a hand held weapon)
- Analog watch (an analog watch can be used as a compass, a digital can't)

As you can see, these items are more focused on self-defense and getting out of your workplace, than they are anything else. The idea isn't so much allowing you to survive in the woods, or even survive sleeping in a cardboard box as you walk home from a disaster. Those items are in your Every Day Carry (EDC) kit. But there are some things that happen so quickly, that waiting till you get to your car just won't work.

If a terrorist or lunatic enters your workplace and starts shooting the place up, you don't have time to go to your car to get your gun. You need to be able to react in seconds. Likewise, if the lights go out, you'll need a flashlight on your person, not in your Every Day Carry (EDC) kit. That's the type of criteria that are used to select these items.

But it's clear that the Every Day Carry (EDC) items listed above aren't going to be enough to get you home, if you have to walk home after an EMP renders your car unusable or some other disaster happens.

There are also many other things that can happen in a day, which really don't qualify as emergencies. Carrying a few basics in your Every Day Carry (EDC) to take care of those little problems is always a great idea.

Every Day Carry (EDC) bags can vary greatly in size, but for most people they're about the size of a lunch box or large fanny pack. I use an over the shoulder bag, but you can use anything. This gives me quite a bit of room for the things I feel I need.

- Shelter - 2 rescue blankets, 20' of para-cord and 10 yd of duct tape
- Rain poncho
- Lifestraw
- Nalgene water bottle
- Some high energy snacks, such as beef jerky, granola bars and nuts
- Spork - useful for those times when my lunch doesn't come with utensils
- Fire starter - I carry a lighter, as well as a BlastMatch Jr. and some WetFire cubes
- Flashlight and spare batteries
- Knife (in addition to the one in my pocket)
- Wire saw

- Compass and map - to help me find my way home
- Lock pick set (ssh!)
- Phone charger - includes cable, adapters for wall and car, as well as a charger battery
- Hair bands - useful as rubber bands for a number of things
- Emergency sewing kit - for quick repairs, heavy on safety pins
- Pen, pencil and waterproof pad
- Photocopies of my driver's license and passport
- Personal hygiene kit - includes antibacterial hand cleaner, disposable toothbrushes, deodorant, 3 compressed towels and Kleenex (can be used as toilet paper)
- First-aid - cloth bandages of various types, abdominal bandages (large bandages) alcohol wipes, cohesive medical tape, antibacterial ointment, pain relievers, antihistamine, 3 day supply of my personal medications, clotting compound and butterfly closures

With this, I have enough to get myself home from pretty much anywhere within walking distance, as well as take care of the problems which might arise during the day. If your work requires you to dress in a way that is not conducive for walking, add good walking shoes and some more comfortable clothes. Always carry a jacket with you, even on days when you don't need it. You might need it at night.

Chapter 6: The Bug Out Bag

When the time comes to bug out, you're going to need equipment and supplies to survive; that's where the bug out bag comes in. You're not going to be able to go to someplace where you can pick up a loaf of bread and a gallon of milk at the corner store. Nor are you likely to find an abandoned cabin in the woods, with a welcome sign hanging on the door.

You're going to have to live off of what you take with you, the knowledge you have and what nature provides. So, it's best to take as much with you as possible while keeping in mind weight, specifically the things that will help you survive out in the wild long-term. Of course, that means knowing how to use those things to survive with as well. Ultimately, the most important thing you can take with you is the knowledge of how to survive.

The bug out bag must provide for all of your basic needs, so it would be a good idea to review what those are. In order of priority, your needs are:

- Safety & Security
- Maintaining your body heat (this includes clothing, shelter and fire)
- Purified water
- Food
- First-aid (including personal hygiene)

Carrying all of that is going to be a bit difficult. You have to assume that you're going to have to go on foot at some point. Even if you leave home in your car or truck, chances are that you'll have to abandon it along the way. With that in mind, you need to make your bug out bag something that you can carry, such as a backpack. While other things can be used, a backpack is your best bet.

When selecting a backpack, try to avoid something that is obviously military in appearance. That's too easy to identify as what it is.

You don't want people to realize that you're bugging out or recognize that you're prepared. So, you're better off with a backpacker's backpack, rather than a military one unless things have gotten completely out of control.

At the same time, if you find yourself in a combat situation prior to heading out a military backpack of some kind may not be a bad option because it is designed with combat as its primary task. You will need something rugged and durable regardless.

Also you'll want to make sure that whatever backpack you pick has a weight-bearing belt. Your legs are much stronger than your back, and can support the weight of the backpack and its contents easier than your back can. But if the pack doesn't have a belt, your back will have to carry the weight and that's a serious no, no.

Most people have to limit their pack to about one-fourth their body weight. But that's assuming that you're in shape. If not, you'll have to make it even less.

One way to compensate for this is to have every member of the family carry their own pack. While women and children can't carry as big or heavy a pack as a man can, they should be able to carry their own clothes, personal toiletries and sleeping bag, as well as some of the communal food.

Bug out bags are very personal, simply because each person's situation is unique. You need to match the pack you carry to your needs, the terrain you are going to travel through, the area you are going to set up camp and your own survival skills. There's absolutely no sense in carrying equipment you can't use, no matter how useful it might seem. Additionally don't forget to leave room for weapons and ammunition – this is one of the most over looked areas of so called experts who advise on building Bug Out Bags. Safety and Security should be the number one thing to consider in your preparedness because without security you will no doubt be a victim in some way, shape, or form.

One small great option to consider for perimeter security is a 12 gage alert. This small item can be attached to a tree and loaded with a blank 12 gage round. When a person or animal walks past and trips the wire it will go off.

Now because of the nature of this device and the legality of such I have to throughout a disclaimer to use according to all Federal, State, and local laws. Also please be advised that if you add any type of actual "Live Rounds" even less then lethal rounds you will be breaking some serious Federal laws – Do you own research prior to modifying this device in anyway and only use it according to its indented purpose. Now if SHTF is occurring and the United States is no longer a functional government you may want to re-evaluate things based on the current dynamics going on. Again Your Decision, Your Responsibilities, and Your possible Consequences.

Chapter 7: What To Buy

A Basic Shopping List for Your BOB

Basic Tools for your Bug out Bag: The Concept: Never rely completely on one particular item to get a job done!

- Back Pack
- Your Weapons & Ammo (a Ruger 10/22 or Shotgun is a Great Choice for general survival but will only help a little when dealing with the two legged bad guys – for that consider the AR15, AK, or SKS.
- Good Knife (The Best You Can Afford)
- Multi-Function Tool (Gerber or Leatherman)
- Folding Saw (Bahco Laplander)
- Bob's Quick Buck Saw (with extra blades)
- One Gransfors Bruks Axe
- Cold Steel Special Forces Shovel
- 550 Cord 300 feet and number 12 Bank Line (1lb spoil)

Shelter:

- Small 2 person Tent. This is actually a one-person tent with your gear. If you have a family plan accordingly. However, just remember to stay out of sight. Reusable Space Emergency Blanket / Tarp
- SOL Emergency Bivy – Green
- United States Military Bivy is another option. This is more durable but add a little more weight.
- One 100% Wool Blanket. Make sure it's actually 100% wool.

Fire Starting Equipment:

- Faro Rod
- Magnifying Glass
- Flint & Steel
- Metal Container holding Card Cloth
- Matches in water proof container of some kind
- Lighters
- Knowledge and Ability to start fire using primitive techniques such as the bow and drill & hand drill and Modern Techniques of using Batteries to start fires.

Food:

- Cliff Bars (20 grams of Protein each)
- Organic Trail Mix
- 1 Mainstay Food Ration Bar (3600 cal.)
- 3-5 MREs (because you don't need water to cook them)
- Snares, Fishing Yo Yos, and two 220 Conibear Traps
- The Ability to catch, trap, or hunt game to secure a renewable food source as well as process it in the field. Don't forget to bring some zip lock bags. Learn how to smoke you meats to help preserve it.

Water:

- Water Filter (Katadyn filter)
- 1 Plastic fold-down 5 gallon water container w/ Purification Tablets
- 1 Steel cup/bowl for boiling water (Stanley put out a really good little kit)
- Knowledge and Ability to gather and create safe drinking water through creating a Solar Still, Survival Filter, and Boiling Water

Documents:

- Small Bible
- Small copy of Declaration of Independence and US Constitution with Bill of Rights
- Small survival field book
- And of course maps of locations you will be traveling in.

Chapter 8: Conclusion

The conclusion of this book is actually the beginning of your journey. Now is the time to take massive action and get things done but not out of the spirit of fear, but out of a spirit of love.

We have covered some critical areas of survival throughout this book. I hope that you use this book as it's intended, for the purpose of this book is for you and your family to get as prepared as possible by giving you the knowledge of prepping and survival basics.

Special Gift

God has a Gift for You!   The Plan of
Salvation:

There is no formal prayer of salvation as
many churches would have you believe,
God's Word is very clear - there is only one
way to get to the Father in heaven and that is
through Jesus Christ (John 14:6). Jesus says
that you must be born again to enter into
heaven (John 3:3-5).

Salvation is simply the first step in building
an open and honest relationship with God.
We all have sinned and fall short every day,
but there is Hope in Jesus Christ - Just cry
out to God in sincerity and honesty asking
for forgiveness and for Him to Save you,
Sanctify you, and fill you with His Holy
Spirit - Ask for His will to be done in your
life on earth as it is in Heaven and That's it,
now just keep it real with God.

A Warning:

The Christian walk is not an easy life on the surface. The Word of God says that we will be hated in all the world for Christ namesake (Matt. 24:9). The Bible says that in the last days are enemy prevail against us physically until Christ returns to save us (Dan 7:21, 22). Furthermore, we must endure hardship as a good soldier of Jesus Christ (2 Tim 2:3) and yet we are never alone in this, God promises us that He will never leave us nor forsake us if we believe in him (Matt.28:20).

In everything we go through we have the peace and joy of God which surpasses all understanding (Philp. 4:6-8) The Bible declares, "For I consider the sufferings of this present time are not worthy to be compared with the glory which shall be revealed in us". (Rom 8:18). However, in all these things we are more than conquerors through Jesus Christ (Rom. 8:37)

Stay In Contact

Our Contact Information

Stay in Contact with the American Christian Defense Alliance, Inc. Contactus@acdainc.org Or Email Us Though Our Website At: www.ACDAInc.Org

Join Our Mailing List

We also Greatly Appreciate You Signing Up For Our Mailing List and Providing a Good Rating and review for this Book. Your reviews help other people like yourself find this book on Amazon and benefit from its contents.

If You or Your Family have been Blessed by this book please let us know by dropping us a line through our website at http://acdainc.org

Thanks Again for Reading

God Bless!

Find All Our Books On Amazon

Our Books on Amazon:

Biblical Bug Out: Don't Bug In - Follow The Calling

Christian Prepping 101: How To Start Prepping

Prepping: A Christian Perspective

Bug Out: Preparations

Real Men Don't Make Promises: Understanding Oaths, Pacts, Covenants & Promises From A Biblical Perspective

A Vague Notion: How To Overcome Limiting Beliefs of Fear and Anxiety Through the Word of God

Dirt on Your Tabies: 7 Short Stories of Seisho Ryu Ninjutsu

Salvation for Your Unsaved Mom: 10 Things to Tell Your Mom Before She Dies

www.ingramcontent.com/pod-product-compliance
Lightning Source LLC
Chambersburg PA
CBHW022132280326
41933CB00007B/649